THE MUSHROOM OVER HIROSHIMA

And the life of one youth in its aftermath

by
Reiko Odate Matsumoto

FOREWORD

Life in Hiroshima during World War II and its aftermath was chaotic. The atomic bomb the United States dropped on the city on August 6, 1945, was devastating. Sixty-six thousand people were killed, and sixty-nine thousand were injured. Three days later, in Nagasaki, on the southern island of Kyushu, another bomb was dropped, killing thirty-nine thousand people and injuring twenty-five thousand more. This story is a fiction based on factual events. The facts and figures were researched from *The Atomic Bombings of Hiroshima and Nagasaki*, by the Manhattan Engineer District, June 29, 1946.

The purpose of this book is to help readers understand how the people of the city coped in the war's aftermath. It describes Japan's way of life as it was then. It focuses on one youth, whose aspirations for the future were destroyed by the war and then regained through a simple truth.

ACKNOWLEDGMENTS

My husband, Hisao, spent his early childhood and teen years in Hiroshima and supplied me with many of the details of life then. My visits to the city and to his home further deepened my appreciation for the way of the Japanese.

My daughter, Marguerite Backhausen, patiently helped to format the document and communicated with the publisher to get the story printed.

Akio Aoyagi, with knowledge of his native Japan, produced the sketches that enhance readers' understanding of the setting.

ABOUT THE AUTHOR AND ILLUSTRATOR

Reiko Odate Matsumoto, author, is a retired elementary-school teacher. She lives in Ashburn, Virginia, with her husband and has three grown children and three grandchildren.

Akio Aoyagi, illustrator, is a retired interior designer and lives in Berkeley, California.

CHAPTER 1

THE MUNITIONS FACTORY

"Hey, what are you doing here? Get up!" The seventeen-year-old youth lying on the concrete floor felt a hard kick on his side. Instantly he got up and confronted a scowling middle-aged man.

"Sensei, I am sorry. I was sleepy. I will get back to work right away." The young boy started to leave, but the man stopped him.

"I'm surprised at you. Don't you know that there is a war on and you must do your share to help the country? No one is allowed to be lazy. Tonight, you must bring your mother to me to apologize for your laziness."

"Yes, Sensei, I understand."

"Now, go back to your station!" commanded the man.

The boy scurried back to the assembly line and continued the tedious work of assembling rifle parts. He avoided the snide looks of his class-mates that seemed to say, *So, you got caught!*

He was troubled. His mother and father were not at home. He and his little brother were home alone while Mother went to the city of Fukuoka on the island of Kyushu to pick up Father at the hospital. Now he would have explain to Tanaka Sensei and explain the situation.

The year was 1945. Japan and America were both caught in World War II and the Pacific Campaign was now in its fourth year. All Japanese middle-school boys and girls were forced to work in factories making rifles and war gear. Schoolteachers who were too old to be conscripted into the Imperial Army were relegated to positions as factory managers and foremen. The man who had awakened the youth was Tanaka Sensei, the math teacher of the boy's middle school. The munitions factory had once been a place where construction equipment was made. After the war, it would be used to make Mazda automobiles.

It was dark when the youth and his younger brother returned home. They started to cook rice in the *kama* kettle sitting in the *kamado*, a clay stove with a hole in its surface. The floor of the kitchen was packed mud, but clean. On one side of the kitchen was a raised platform with a low table. Around the table were cushions to sit on. When the rice was done, they removed it from the *kamado* and set it aside to steam. They placed another *kama* in the opening. The younger boy kept the fire stoked with firewood they had gathered from the woods behind their house a few days earlier. The youth pumped water from the well in the courtyard and poured it into the *kama*. He put four little dried anchovies into the pot and then placed unpeeled carrots, potatoes,

Kamado

beans, and cabbage in to make a stew. Then the two sat before the family Buddhist altar. Their parents had strictly enforced the habit of everyone reciting a short sutra before the evening meal. Once, when the youth was younger, he had refused to do this and had not been allowed to eat the meal. When the stew was done, they ladled it into two individual bowls, along with the rice, and the two boys sat at the table, put their hands together, bowed their heads, and said, "*Itadaki masu,* I gratefully receive this food."

After they had finished dinner, the boys cleaned the kitchen, put the dishes away, and prepared for bed. They slid open the door of a deep closet and got out two heavy futon quilts and dragged them onto the tatami straw-mat floor. They got the sheets and a lighter quilt for a blanket. They sat on the tatami before the Buddhist altar and chanted another sutra, then said *oyasumi nasai,* good night, and went to bed.

Early the next morning, after putting their bedding away, the boys made their *hinomaru* lunches of rice balls with a red plum in the center to resemble the Japanese flag. They wrapped the rice balls in dried, clean bamboo leaves. They longed for the flavored seaweed wafers usually used to wrap rice balls, but in the war, that was a luxury not to be had. They were fortunate that they could grow their own

Rice Balls

rice and vegetables, unlike many in their city of Hiroshima and in other cities.

Although they grew their rice in their own rice paddies, they were allowed to keep only some of it for themselves; they had to give the rest to the co-op so others could have their rice rations. They were not allowed to eat white rice, so the boys put the brown rice in a widemouthed jar and, with a long-handled spoon, pushed down on the brown kernels many times to get the rough brown husks off. They found this more palatable than the rough brown rice.

RICE FIELDS

Mother had circled the date, August 6, on the calendar, and said, "We'll be home this day. You'll take care of yourselves for two days, won't you?"

Before leaving for the factory, the boys crossed the narrow path in front of their house to the garden at the foot of a hilly slope and gathered mulberry leaves to feed the hungry silkworms that were housed in the shed. Like many women in the area, their mother would later boil the cocoons and then spin the silk, which she would also gather from the other families, into parachutes. Everyone helped the war effort in his or her way.

It was seven o'clock when they reported for work. The youth and his classmates had been at their station for an hour and a half when they heard planes overhead, and the familiar siren for them to duck and cover.

They were sure that American planes would drop propaganda leaflets over the city again. They had had such air raid warnings before and although the big cities nearby had been bombed, Hiroshima never had been and they had felt lucky. But this time, they saw a bright light and felt a hard jolt and heard the sounds of breaking glass and falling slate. This jolt was like nothing they had felt before. The youth felt something hard hit his head. Plaster and dust and pieces of glass were all around him. Someone shouted, "Hiroshima City's been hit!"

They all rushed outside and saw the devastation around them. Pieces of slate from the roof, and shards of glass and wood from the shattered windows, lay on the ground.

The teachers shouted, "Everyone, go home and see if your families and homes are safe." The youth looked for his younger brother and found him looking frightened. He grabbed his hand, and together they rushed toward their home.

No one at that time knew of the horrible devastation wreaked by a bomb so powerful and evil. Someone shouted, "Look, there's a strange cloud over the city. It looks like a giant mushroom." They all knew that something awful had happened and that they needed to go home, where it would be safe.

The two boys raced to their home, over two miles away. They found the gate to the courtyard askew, and when they stepped in, they looked

COURTYARD

in horror at the pieces of glass, the gray roof tiles, and the broken sliding doors on the courtyard ground. The shed where they kept their store of food and the silkworms leaned precariously to one side, though the walls were intact. They breathed a sigh of relief to know that although the house was damaged, for the most part it had withstood the blast.

But where were their parents? They should have been home by now, as they were to take the overnight train from Fukuoka City, and Hiroshima Station was just two miles from their home. Had they been in the city when it was bombed?

The youth said, "We must go and look for Mother and Father. Father is too weak to walk; we can carry him."

Without thinking of their own danger, the two boys raced toward the city. Everywhere they walked, there was shattered wood, mortar, slate tiles, and glass. An adult stopped them. "Boys, go back to your home. You must not be walking around here—it's too dangerous."

LITTLE GIRL SITTING IN RUINS

"But we need to find our parents," they insisted. They stared at a pile of rubble on the ground a few feet in front of them and realized it was a heap of human bodies smoldering, and heard loud, anguished moans from all around. Were their parents in that heap? Were the cries their cries?

"No, go home, and wait for them. If they're all right, they'll be back."

Dejectedly, the two boys turned around and returned home. They sobbed quietly, clinging to each other.

The youth said to his brother, "Let's clean up as much as we can. Get the rake and broom; we'll start with the front yard." So the two swept up the glass and piled up the wood and cleared a path to the house. There was little damage inside the house. The shoji sliding doors had fallen, and some glass had broken, but they were able to put the shoji up again. Upstairs, they saw a gaping hole in the roof where some of the slate tiles had blown off.

Suddenly, they heard, "Oh, boys, you are all right!" It was their mother. They rushed to their parents, and they all clung to one another. They were about to hear a horrible tale of that awful day.

CHAPTER 2

PICA DON

THE BRIGHT LIGHT, THE FRIGHTENING SOUND

Sekiyo was eager to return to her home on the outskirts of Hiroshima City that very hot and humid morning in August 1945. Her husband sat in the seat next to her on the slow overnight train from Fukuoka City on the island of Kyushu. He had been released from Fukuoka Hospital, as there was no cure for the cancer that was eating his stomach. She had gone to pick him up to take him home to spend the rest of his living days there. When they arrived at Hiroshima Station, her husband stepped onto the platform and gazed lovingly at the city and sighed in contentment. "Such a beautiful city, I'm so happy to be home. Yes, it's good to be home," he repeated.

There was a tunnel connecting the two opposite sides of the railway. "Let's sit in the tunnel and rest awhile. We still have a bus ride

RESTING IN TUNNEL

before we get home," said Sekiyo. They walked down the stairs slowly and lowered their bags onto the concrete floor, but before they could sit on the cold floor, they were blinded by a bright light that shot down the stairwell from above.

The couple stared at each other. "What could that *pika* light be? I'll go above to look."

As Sekiyo climbed the concrete steps, she felt an eerie silence, then heard the *don* sounds: the crashing, the shattering, the sound of metal on metal. When she reached the platform, all was flat around her. The trains were crushed, with people crushed in them, the roof of the train station had collapsed, and there were no tall buildings standing anywhere, except

ATOMIC DOME

the dome which housed the Hiroshima Chamber of Commerce, which was beginning to emit red flames into the sky. Then she heard the cries of human pain and anguish.

She rushed down the steps. "Hurry, we must get home to see if the boys are all right," she urged her husband. They ran up the steps on the opposite side of the station and made for the street. There were no buses, only crushed metal and human bodies strewn about. They headed in the direction of their home, ignoring the sights of human suffering along the way.

Once, as Sekiyo glanced back, she saw a huge cloud rising from the flattened city. "That cloud, that cloud, it looks like a mushroom!" Fear gripped their hearts as they gazed at the ominous unknown specter and the fires that glowed from all directions. But they continued their flight toward home.

On that long train ride home from Fukuoka the night before, they had reminisced about their life together. It had begun thirty-five years ago, when

RUSHING HOME

she had taken a long boat trip to America to marry a man she had never met. He had just lost his wife and was looking for a young, healthy woman who would be his helpmate and give him many sons. Sekiyo had been approached by a relative, and she had accepted. This was the way marriages were arranged then in Japan. She was a risk taker, an adventurer, young, and eager to explore the world.

Life in America was hard—the food, the customs, the hard work. But they had persevered. Their life together started in Seattle, Washington, and then they moved to Superior, in southern Wyoming. There, they bought a laundry to serve the workers of the coal-mining town. They experienced freezing cold winters, where the winds were relentless, and blazing hot summers, where the dust and wind were endless. On cold mornings, Sekiyo had to scrub the miners' clothes, black with coal dust, in the chilly morning air, then hang them to dry. In the winters, the clothes would freeze and the stiff laundry then must be ironed to dry.

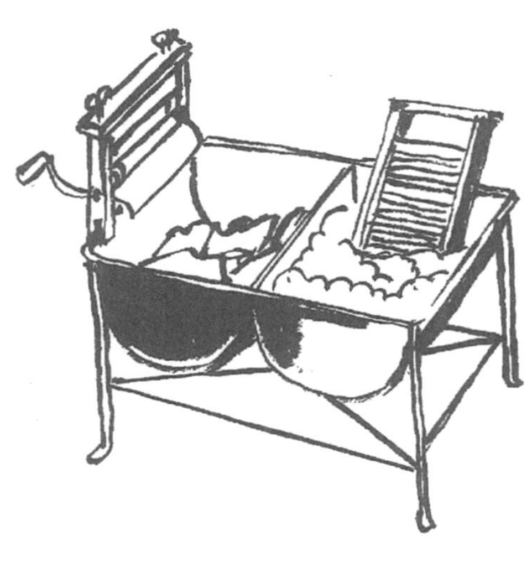

In the summers, the dust would make the clothes even dirtier. But they survived, and managed to make enough so that Sekiyo's husband could buy a Ford Model T.

Life seemed good, except for their unhappiness that they had no children. The local doctor in Rock Springs, the closest big city, told Sekiyo that she had breast cancer and that she must go to Denver, Colorado, to see a specialist. She did that on long bus rides, hardly able to speak English, but she was determined to cure her illness and have many children. She encountered kindness everywhere she went. In the big city of Denver, a policeman escorted her across the street as she attempted to cross it. Somehow, she survived the surgery, made her way back to Superior, and continued the arduous labor of laundering.

After eight years, they sold their business, packed their belongings in the Ford Model T that her husband had managed to buy, and left for Los Angeles, California. They found jobs working on a flower farm. In California, the couple had a son who gave them endless joy. They were eager to show this precious child to their aging parents in Japan, so they returned to their home country for what they thought was to be a short visit. Sekiyo, in her wisdom, made sure that they all had visas to return to America.

But this was not to be. Their elderly parents begged them to remain, and thus they were in Japan on that fateful day when their country bombed the ships in Pearl Harbor, in the US territory of Hawaii, and began the long war years of suffering that followed.

Now, on August 6, 1945, their only thought was for the safety of their two boys as they rushed to their home on the outskirts of the city, four miles away. They were relieved to see that much of the suburbs had been spared the devastation and many of the familiar buildings were intact. They rushed up the short slope to their home and pushed open the courtyard gate.

"Mother, Father, what happened? We were so worried," the boys greeted them. The family stood in an embrace, happy to see one another unharmed.

"Did you see the planes?" The two boys were eager to know.

"It's been so long, I thought of you two each day in the hospital," their father said weakly.

"We thought about you too, and we're so glad that you're finally home, but, Mother, tell us what you saw."

Mother turned to the Buddhist altar, lit a candle and some incense sticks, rang the little bell three times, bowed low before the image of Buddha, and said, "Thank you for keeping our children and us safe."

Sekiyo wiped tears from her eyes as if trying to wipe away the horrible sights she had encountered: the burned bodies that she had stepped over, the cries of help that she had ignored as she half-carried her husband toward their home. Then she told them the story of what they had experienced at the train station.

CHAPTER 3

HIBAKUSHA

THE VICTIMS

Bang, bang. "Help, let us in!"

The four of them looked toward the gate to the courtyard, where the cries were coming from. Without hesitation, the youth rushed to the gate. When he opened it, he gasped at the sight before him. Who were these people?

"Don't you know us? I'm Fumiko, your cousin Kenta's wife," the woman implored. Her body was covered with blood from her arms. On her back was an old woman, probably her mother, also covered with blood.

Sekiyo rushed forward, "My, Fumiko-san, please, come in, come in. Hurry, son, get some water—we must make them comfortable."

The boy rushed to get a washbasin, went to the pump, and returned with water.

Sekiyo quickly washed Fumiko's arms and, pulling off her burned sleeves, gazed in horror at the burned skin that now was peeling off with the fabric. The old woman who had been on the younger woman's back had slid off and now lay on the ground, ominously silent, with her eyes wide open.

They all gazed at the body, now lifeless, and realized that she was dead. Sekiyo and her husband, the rest following, put their hands together and recited, "*Namo Amida Butsu.*"

"She is at peace," said their father. He gently covered her body with a sheet, and, with heads bowed, they chanted a Buddhist sutra for the body's safe journey to Nirvana.

No sooner had they raised their heads than they heard another cry for help outside the courtyard gate. Outside stood a line of twelve or more people—men, women, children, babies—all covered with blood, skin peeling from their faces. "Please help us," the man who seemed to be the leader implored.

"Of course, of course, come in, come in," said Sekiyo, as she motioned for them to enter the courtyard.

They recognized some of the people as distant relatives or friends of relatives, but some were complete strangers. Sekiyo recognized two ladies as women who had asked her for help with *senninbari* a few months earlier. The women were gathering one stitch each from friends and relatives until they had collected a thousand stitches on a scarf.

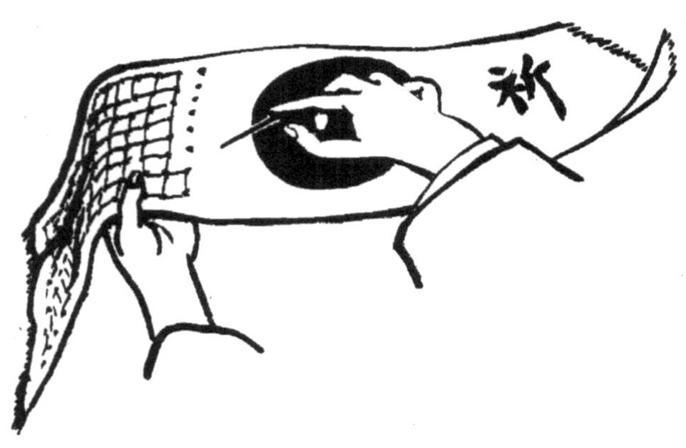

Seninbari

Sekiyo had willingly made her one stitch on each scarf. They would then present the scarves to a departing warrior. The soldiers would tie the scarves around their necks or around their torso to ward off bullets and shrapnel, a "bulletproof vest" made of the thoughts of a thousand people to protect them. This practice was carried out throughout Japan; the empress herself had stitched many a scarf.

After letting the last of the people in, the youth quickly bolted the front gate, but not until he caught a glimpse of more people going to neighbors' doors, banging on them and begging for help.

"Boys, pull out all the futons and bedding from the closets and lay them on the floor. We must make these people comfortable."

When everyone had a spot to lie on, all three of the large tatami rooms were covered with injured people sleeping head to toe. Those who could climb the steep stairs were upstairs as well. Sekiyo sent the younger boy to the garden to dig some sweet potatoes. She cut the tubers and added them to rice gruel for extra nutrition. She ordered the youth to heat the bathwater. The older boy pumped water and emptied the pail into a large metal kettle. This was their bath-

GOEMONBURO

tub, called a *furo*. This was a *goemon buro*. The boy remembered where the label came from: there was once a famous thief, named Ishikawa Goemon, who hid from his pursuers in such a kettle. In his haste, he did not realize that the wooden rack was out of the kettle, drying. When the homeowner started a fire under the iron kettle, the thief couldn't stand the heat, jumped out, and was thus caught. The boy smiled as he recalled the story, as told by his father many years ago.

The family would scoop hot water from this kettle, scrub themselves, rinse their bodies, then step into the kettle to soak, but not until they were sure that a wooden rack was in place on the floor of the kettle—else they would burn their feet. When the water was heated, Sekiyo painstakingly and lovingly bathed the guests' bodies.

The next morning, Sekiyo woke the boys and declared, "We must do something about disposing of the body of the dead woman, because in this August heat, it will start to decay and smell. We can't burn or bury it here. Go to the priest in the temple on the hill and ask what we should do."

The youth rushed out of the gate, passing corpses that had never made it to help, and ran up the forty-eight stone steps to the temple. He met the priest coming out of the temple, where people lay on the floor of the *hondo*, or main hall.

"Yes, I know, we have decided to designate a cremating spot in the elementary school's playground and burn the bodies there. Bring the Buddha, the deceased, there and we will hold a short service and start the pyre."

The boy returned home and reported this to his parents.

"You and your brother must take the Buddhas there," announced his mother.

Buddhas? wondered the boy. Yes, there had been another death in the short time he was away. This time, it was a child. The boys had never heard the word "Buddha" used to refer to dead bodies, but that was the Buddhist way.

The boys created a makeshift stretcher, placed the old woman and child on it, and walked to the school ground. There, they met others with the same mission. After a short sutra, with all of them clasping their hands together and chanting with bowed heads, some men brought flaming torches and lit the wood piled beneath the bodies. The recurring stench was nothing that anyone had smelled before.

They all covered their noses and mouths and gagged. Then the boys left.

As they sadly walked home, they gazed at the familiar playground of their old elementary school, recalling the happy times they had had there, playing softball and soccer, swinging on the monkey bars, climbing the jungle gym, and playing hide-and-seek. Also, during the war, ladies and children gathered at the playground with handmade bamboo spears to practice spearing and lancing in case of enemy attack. This was done all over Japan, even in the countryside. The bamboo grove on the hill in front of their home was almost denuded from people coming to cut the strong, resilient stalks for their homemade spears.

The youth remembered that he had been so good at pitching that his teachers had urged him to continue to play softball in middle school, but between his father's illness and the work he had to do to help his mother with the rice paddies and garden, he had no time to practice, so that dream had perished.

When they returned home, they were greeted by their mother, whose ashen face revealed that something terrible had happened. "Boys, Nagasaki City in Kyushu has been bombed! When will it all end? Oh, why must we suffer for nothing!" she wailed.

Nagasaki City? wondered the youth. That city, too, had never been bombed before.

Then, on the fifteenth of the month, the emperor of Japan announced on the radio that Japan had surrendered to the United States, that the country had lost the war. Everyone sitting before the radio was silent. Then they all wept. They wept for their lost families, their lost homes, and their lost country. What was to happen now?

KARMA

Each day, the two boys made the trip to the community cremation spot as their patient guests died—many of them painfully, others silently in their sleep.

Not only had they had to endure the stench of burning flesh, but at home and in the neighborhood, the putrid smell that the rotting, burned flesh and the overflowing outhouses emitted attracted thousands of flies and mosquitoes. Just to fan them away was a task. All the neighbors wore cotton scarves over their faces to keep the stench away. Day after day, the smell hovered over the countryside like a low-hanging cloud that never disappeared.

Early in September, their neighbor Mrs. Takata came breathlessly to their home to announce the good news that her nephew Shoji, in the next village, had returned from the war unharmed. His parents had received word that he had died in a suicide plane attack, and had held a memorial for him. At age twenty-one, he was a kamikaze pilot.

KAMIKAZE

They were proud to have given their son to their country. But he had returned! They found him one morning huddled outside their courtyard gate. It seemed his plane, which was ready to take off, was found to be defective, and while it was being repaired, the war was declared over. In the confusion that followed, no one had thought to notify his family. Shoji himself was ashamed and chagrined that he was not able to die for his country, but of course his family was elated.

They all knew of the origin of the word *kamikaze*, or "wind gods." Many centuries ago, the Mongols from far-off Mongolia were about to invade southern Japan, or the Kyushu islands. But while they were sailing in their ships in the strait separating Korea from Japan, strong winds sank all the ships, and thus Japan was saved by the wind gods, or *kamikaze*. This term was applied to the suicide bombers during the war.

One day in October, the boys noticed that their father was especially weak, not caring to eat or drink. They summoned the village doctor, but he could do nothing.

"You need to let him be at peace; there is nothing anyone can do for him" was the doctor's advice.

In the morning, when the boys got up, they found their mother beside their father's futon, silently chanting a sutra. She was tearless. "He is finally at peace," she whispered. They took him not to the community cremation spot, but to the village crematorium. They placed their father's urn on the Buddhist altar. The following week, they trekked up the hill to the family gravesite beside a bamboo grove and said their final good-byes. The boys' hearts were heavy. They missed their kind, gentle father.

That night, the three sat before the altar and talked about him and reminded each other of all the good times they had had. The youth remembered that at around age five, when the go-cart that they had brought back from America was stolen, their father comforted him by saying, "Don't be angry. Some little boy who never had such a nice thing is enjoying it now. Let's wish him a good time."

The new year festivities normally held in all Japanese homes were not to be this year. Food was scarce, and they could not make the *mochi* rice cakes that they had always made on New Year's Eve. A rice cake soup called *ozoni* was the traditional breakfast fare on New Year's morning. The boys recalled that on days before the end of each year, their mother steamed some sweet rice in a large makeshift steamer she set up in the courtyard, and when

MOCHI MAKING

the sweet rice was done, she hurriedly placed the hot, steaming ball of rice into a mortar made of stone, the *usu*, and their father and the older boy took turns pounding the ball of glutinous rice in a rhythmic fashion with wooden mallets, or *kine*. Their mother turned the hot rice ball between pounds. If the rhythm were broken, her hands could get crushed.

But now there was no *ozoni*. When people came to call on New Year's Day, as was the custom, the family had nothing to offer their guests in the way of *osechi*, or New Year's delicacies. Sekiyo, too, called on her neighbors and friends to thank them for their kindness in the past year and to wish them a good new year. Life in the suburb of Fuchu in Hiroshima continued: the cold winter came, and many of their guests left to look for their old homes; only a few, who had no place to go, remained. Spring came, but schools did not reopen on April 1, the traditional school opening day. The buildings were being repaired, and new teachers were being recruited.

The few people still in their home helped the boys climb up the hill near the gravesite to dig up young bamboo shoots. The bamboo grove had somewhat recovered its over harvesting by the village people. Sekiyo would strip the shoots of their tough husks, boil the tender shoots, and then soak them in water, which she changed daily. Then, at the right time, she would prepare *takenoko gohan*, a pilaf made of bamboo shoots and rice.

Later in the spring, when it was time to plant the rice seedlings, the boys and their mother waded in the muddy paddy and did the backbreaking work of placing the seedlings in neat little rows. Then they waited for the *tsuyu*, summer rains, to flood the paddies so the seedlings could grow. They started their kitchen garden and planted their cabbage, soybeans, radish, tomatoes, cucumbers, and potatoes. In the fall, they gathered the rice plants, winnowed the grains, packed them in bags, and hung the straw to dry.

Now that the war was over, Sekiyo and other women in the neighborhood were spared the task of growing silkworms and spinning the silk. It was not imperative anymore, as there was no need for silk parachutes. Sekiyo instructed the youth to store her spinning wheel in the air raid shelter that the boys and their father had dug in the side of the hill in front of their home. They had never had to use the shelter, although they had rushed to it at the sound of the air raid siren.

One day, while the youth was at the vegetable vendor, he heard some men's loud, angry voices. He heard them talking about the bombing and declaring, "The United States used us as experimental rats! They did not bomb Hiroshima and Nagasaki because they had planned to drop the atomic bomb and study the results of the new bomb. If the city had been bombed before, there would not have been any way of knowing whether the damage had already been there, so they needed cities that were still 'clean.'

The youth was stunned. So that was it! He had wondered all along why they had not been bombed like Tokyo, Kobe, and Osaka. He rushed home to inform his mother of what he had heard. She confirmed that fact. "A few of us suspected it," she replied, but said nothing more.

"Aren't you angry?" asked the youth.

She looked at him. "*Shikata ga nai.* It can't be helped, it was war, this is our karma. We must accept it."

He had heard her recite this like a mantra many times before, and wondered why his people were so fatalistic.

CHAPTER 5

THE BEGINNING OF A NEW LIFE

Life continued as before, but there was despair in the youth's heart. "Mother, what shall I do with my life? I barely finished junior high school, and I can't seem to pass the entrance exam to the national high school. We can't afford to send me to a private high school, and if I can't go to high school, I'll never be able to find decent work to support us."

It was now nine months since the horrible day in August, and try as he might, the youth, now seventeen years old, was unable to concentrate on studying for the entrance to Hiroshima National High School. Education for all of Japan from grades one to six was compulsory and free, but middle school and high school attendance was optional. Those who could pass the stringent exams could enter the national middle and high schools free, but those who could not went to private schools if they could afford to. If not, they joined the workforce in their community.

The city was beginning to rebuild itself, but the youth was too young for the required heavy construction work, and work in his family's fields and garden kept him occupied. He aspired for more. He desperately wanted to continue his education. He found himself frustrated, angry, bored, and tired of caring for sick people and of working in the garden and rice paddies. He dreamed of going to Tokyo and going to the Imperial University. But he couldn't study, for he had no books and no time, and he knew he could never pass the difficult entrance exams.

One evening after dinner, his mother called him to the family Buddhist altar and told him something he had never known. She brought out a little book called a passport and showed him that he was an American citizen.

PASSPORT

The youth was stunned. He was an American citizen and had not known it until now. During the war with America, if his friends had known he was American, he may have been bullied. He silently thanked his parents for their wisdom. After returning to Japan, his mother had become pregnant, and so his younger brother was a Japanese citizen.

"Sixteen years ago, when we left America for Japan, I got return visas to that wonderful country. When it was time to leave Japan, Father's parents begged us to stay, as they were aging and needed our help. We could not refuse, so we stayed. All these years, your father and I did not tell you or anyone else about the return visas or your citizenship. I was nervous all the years of the war, as you were getting close to the age of military conscription. Had you been drafted into the Japanese army, I would have had to disclose your American citizenship. You would have lost it and would never be able to return to the country of your birth."

The youth hesitated. "But Americans hate Japanese. They imprisoned all of them, put them in prisons, and stole their homes and money. I won't go where I'll be hated and treated like a slave!"

Sekiyo reassured him that since the war was over, things in America had changed. They talked long into the night. She related her story of going to a big city called Denver all by herself, hardly able to speak English, to have an operation for her breast cancer. She was treated kindly by everyone, and she remembered a policeman helping her cross the street.

The very next day, Sekiyo walked two miles to visit an old friend who had been in America at the same time she was. Early that afternoon, she hurriedly returned to tell the youth of good news. Mrs. Nakano had told her that her American nephew was in the American occupation forces based at Sasebo Naval Base on Kyushu, and would be visiting her in a few days. She would ask him for help in some way.

One weekend, the family was surprised to see a stranger, clearly Japanese, but an American soldier, judging by the uniform he wore, approach their home. He spoke Japanese with ease and explained that his family remaining in California would be happy to sponsor the youth. He explained that there would be some paperwork to do, but because the youth still had his citizenship, the trip to the American consulate would be simple.

It took a whole year after that visit for everything to work out. The youth was worried; he knew no English except for the few words that his mother remembered and taught him. But Sekiyo reassured him that she and his father, too, knew no English when they went to America, but America was a kind place and people helped in any way they could. She showed him a receipt from the night school she attended to learn English as a second language. It stated DO NOT DESTROY THIS RECEIPT, and she had kept it carefully stowed among her valuables. She also got out some books of English lessons that she had kept all these years, and together they studied from them.

One day, they had three unusual visitors. Two were clearly Caucasian Americans, but one was a fluent-English-speaking Japanese, who was their translator. They identified themselves as members of the ABCC, or Atomic Bomb Casualty Commission inspectors. They asked to talk to one of the family's remaining guests. They made notes as they inquired about how far the person had been from the explosion's epicenter and what kind of wounds he had received, and asked many other personal questions. Sekiyo told them of her experiences, and they told her that since she had escaped before the black rain that had befallen the city a few minutes after the blast, she had not received any radiation. They informed all in the group that everyone in or near the city would have free medical care for life. The Japanese government would pay for it, and they should all register for help.

One day, the youth received the good news that his necessary papers were in order and that he was free to travel to America. Though his joy was powerful, it was coupled with fear and apprehension about his new adventure. Could he face the unknown alone? He had never been on his own before, never even out of the city of Hiroshima. How could he do this? What would happen to his mother and younger brother? He almost changed his mind, and told his mother so. Sekiyo reprimanded him for being such a weakling and said she would be all right; so would his brother.

When the day of his departure neared, he went into the city of Hiroshima for a last look. He was amazed at the reconstruction that had taken place. The streets had been cleared, the buses and trains were running, and tall buildings were now where burned structures had stood a few years back. But the dome, now called the A-Bomb Dome, was as it had been then: charred, and just a skeleton. It would remain so forever to remind all of the devastation that caused it to be so.

Near it hung strings of folded paper cranes, something a little twelve-year-old girl named Sadako had started. She had been told that when she finished her thousandth crane, she would be cured of the leukemia that was ravaging her blood. But she never made it; she died after she had completed her 655th crane. Now people from all over the country and the world were sending folded cranes, and there they hung.

PAPER CRANES

One day, the youth decided to visit an old school friend who lived near the Inland Sea, the famed Seto Naikai. He boarded a train and went just three stops to a town called Seto, and called on his friend. They walked along the shore of the tranquil Inland Sea, watching the gentle waves as they lapped against the shore. He gazed at an island in the middle of the lakelike sea, and with a heavy heart felt he would no longer be able to see any sight so beautiful: the glass-like blue water gleaming in the sun, the oyster racks gently rocking with the breeze, the children playing in the sand. "I don't think I'll see this in America," he said, and that thought saddened him.

His friend rebuked him, "Look to the future. You have had the pleasure of this beautiful sight—you must look forward to another horizon just as lovely."

The following day he decided to visit another classmate, who lived near Miyajima, the famous Island of the Gods. After several bus rides and a short train ride, he arrived in the town of Miyajima. From there, he and his friend took a ferry across the Inland Sea to a small island. The island was supposed to be one of the top three most beautiful places in Japan. It was home to Itsukushima Shrine, which included an orange *torii* gate, that during high tide locked as though it were floating.

The two youths walked down a path lined with stone lanterns, which were supposed to light the way for the gods to arrive at the shrine. They fed the deer that came nuzzling up to them. They recalled how chagrined they had been during the war when because of their work in the factory, they had not been able to participate in a swim across the channel from the mainland However, they did run a five-kilometer race along the coast of the Inland Sea in their first year.

A few weeks later, with his one-way fare to America, the youth and his mother headed for the port city of Kobe. He was to leave on a ship, the *General Gordon*. Hiroshima was a big city, but Kobe was even bigger!

As he stood on the deck, waving to his mother, he feared he would never see her or his city again. Tears of sadness and loneliness trickled down his cheeks. But little did he know then that in three short years he would return to Japan as an American Airman. A week later, as the ship glided under the beautiful red Golden Gate of San Francisco in America, he knew that this was the magic portal to his new life, and to his American dream.

GOLDEN GATE BRIDGE